This is a self help tool to help you find mindfulness in your every day life.

Flip to any page and you'll find a technique that could help.

You've got this!
You're a superhero!

Count: 1, 2, 3, 4, 5, 6, 7, 8, 9, 10

Breathe in and hold:1,2,3
Breathe out.

(Repeat 5 times)

Look around the room, what can you see?

Are there any shapes? How many?

What colours can you see?

How many different colours are there?

Place your hand on your belly and notice with every breath, your hand rise and fall.

Close your eyes and concentrate on this for 20 breaths.

Pick a finger.

Tap that finger on other fingers. Count as you go.

See how many times you can tap each finger.

Place your hand on your chest.

Pat your chest in a circle motion.

Breathe in and out slowly 5 times.

Find all the circles
in the room.

Count as many
as you can.

Count: 10, 9, 8, 7,
6, 5, 4, 3, 2, 1

Count: 1, 2, 3, 4, 5,
6, 7, 8, 9, 10

Breathe in as
deep as you can.

Hold. Breathe out. Repeat.

Place your hands on your chest and belly.

What noises can you hear?
Is there a bird?
Someone talking?

Count how many different noises you can hear.

What are

5 things you can see?

4 things you can feel?

3 things you can hear?

2 things you can smell?

Think of a song.

Sing it in your head
or out loud.

Concentrate on the lyrics.
Notice what's around
you while you sing.

Are there colours?

Remember:

**You've got this!
You are strong!
You're a superhero!**

www.ingramcontent.com/pod-product-compliance
Lightning Source LLC
Chambersburg PA
CBHW061808290426
44109CB00031B/2971